FOLLOW THE THREAD

This catalog is the culmination of one of my favorite examples of unanticipated discoveries that happen in community based museums. We were approached by the fine volunteer researchers of the Arizona Quilt Documentation Project and Arizona Quilt Study Group who asked to view our quilt collection for inclusion in their efforts to inventory quilts statewide. Their first visit revealed that our holdings were highly significant as a survey of styles, materials and chronology in Arizona. Their subsequent visits included volunteers and Museum staff carefully inspecting, documenting and photographing the entire collection. We uncovered wonderful examples of quilting and fascinating stories of how the quilts made their way to Wickenburg. This information was added to our collections database and will assist research for generations to come.

The wealth of information led us to create the exhibition *Follow the Thread: Quilts from the Museum's Permanent Collection* which was installed in four rotations in our Cultural Crossroads Learning Center throughout 2016. We chose these four groupings to organize the pieces:

"Red!" explored various reds found in American quilts through the 19th and 20th centuries.

"Femininity" reflected on quilting intertwined with women's history. Examples illustrated designs and colors often termed feminine. They also represented traditions of quilt making for fairs and charities.

"Preserve or Restore?" shed light on the continuing need for textile preservation or restoration. Quilts in this group needed restoration of some sort to be safely displayed.

"Cultural Influences" explored styles representative of various cultures. Examples included a Log Cabin quilt by a maker of Hispanic descent, Crazy quilts inspired by Japanese crazed vases, and a Wickenburg Album Quilt depicting the local area.

The Vulture Peak Patchers group assisted in preparing pieces to display safely with the encouragement of Elaine Hamm and Kathie Van Winkle. Cassandra Adams, an assistant at the Museum, took on the planning of exhibition rotations and installations as her first exhibition project and along with staff members Mary Ann Igna, John Kyritsis and David Smith made the displays a reality. We received a generous grant from the Arizona Historical Society to support the installation.

Public programming grew from these efforts including Hassayampa Lectures, Book Club discussions and hands-on activities at a free Family Day. We were happy to be part of quilter gatherings with local and national representatives. Our museum stores even got in on the fun carrying products based on our collection and celebrating quilting for the art form that it is.

We hope you enjoy this catalog that is the lasting memory of the year of the quilt at DCWM. We were approached by Lenna DeMarco, Anne Hodgkins and Arizona Quilt Documentation Project Chairperson Lynn Miller with the idea for this book to showcase the collection. They spent months writing and photographing for the project.

The catalog was generously funded by long-time friend and donor to the Museum Bobbye Rogers through the Joel and Roberta Rogers Trust. Bobbye has a special place in her heart for publications and agreed to fund this one without even seeing a draft! We appreciate her confidence in us and unswerving dedication.

Now, *Follow the Thread!*

Sandra Harris
Sandra Harris
Executive Director
Desert Caballeros Western Museum
August 2016

A BRIEF HISTORY OF ARIZONA QUILTING

All text by
Lenna DeMarco (LD) and
Anne Hodgkins (AH)

All photographs by
Lynn Miller

While Arizona officially became a United States Territory in 1863, adventurers and mountain men had been in the area for several decades prior to that. The Butterfield Stage Line began providing service from St. Louis to Tucson in 1858 and it became easier to transport goods and people. Businesses opened to provide services for soldiers, miners, ranchers, farmers and others. The population was clustered around Tucson where there was a legacy of needlework among the female Hispanic population. As the population slowly grew, Anglo-American women arrived with their families or on their own as schoolteachers, dance hall girls or in other occupations. By the 1870s, Mormon settlers arrived in northern Arizona and started ranches, farms and businesses. In 1880, the Southern Pacific Railroad reached Tucson bringing more goods and settlers into the Arizona Territory.

As people came from all over the United States and Europe, they brought with them their customs, aspirations, prejudices and ideals. The women brought their quilts and quilting traditions, too. The pioneer life was harsh and unforgiving. With all they had given up – an active social life for solitude at the homestead; a "proper" house for dugouts or primitive accommodations; abundance of goods for scarcity of everyday necessities; cultural opportunities for isolation – what a comfort it must have been to have a quilt from back home. The women quickly made the best of what they had and whenever possible used their needle and quilting skills to provide clothing and warmth for their families.

Women made utilitarian, simply-designed quilts during Arizona's Territorial period.

Amelia Gilette Haught from Prescott, Arizona Territory constructed a tied "soogan" quilt with an appliquéd sunflower center about 1907 using velvet, wool, corduroy and other fabrics. It is a quilt designed for everyday use out on the range yet its maker took the time to make it lovely. Masterpieces such as Atanacia Santa Cruz Hughes's 1884 silk pineapple quilt and Cora Viola Howell Slaughter and Edith Stowe's circa 1890 "Feather Plumes with Coxcombs" were made.

Closer contact with the rest of the country meant access for Territorial women to more goods including fabric and the availability of publications with needlework ideas and patterns. Quilting "trends" such as Crazy quilts like the Desert Caballeros Western Museum's (DCWM's) "Crazy Quilt with Gold Edge" (p. 8) and red work quilts such as the DCWM's "Embroidered Red Work Summer Spread" (p. 22) were embraced by Arizona's quilters.

Follow the Thread: Quilts from the Desert Caballeros Western Museum Collection

Arizona became the 48th state on February 14, 1912 with an economy based on climate, cattle, cotton, citrus and copper. With statehood Arizona women gained suffrage eight years before the 19th Constitutional Amendment was ratified nationally. Other minority groups such as Hispanics, Native Americans and Asian Americans still had little political power.

Soon Arizona's citizens were involved in World War I. Many women expressed their patriotism through their red, white and blue quilts. Quilts such as the "Red Cross" quilt made by the Pythian Sisters in Phoenix in 1918 were modeled after the fund-raising pattern printed in the December 1917 issue of *The Modern Priscilla*.

By 1930 Arizona had grown to 435,573 people but the Great Depression was about to hit the state very hard. Unemployment and falling prices for the state's agricultural and industrial products made the time particularly difficult. Like other quilt makers across America, Arizona women used feed, flour, sugar, tobacco and salt sacks as well as fabric scraps to construct quilts similar to the DCWM's "Four Patch" quilt (p. 28). Homemakers' groups and county extension services encouraged quilting which provided both a practical and lovely result as well as a social outlet. Quilting was firmly established in the state's minority populations and embraced into their respective cultures.

Possessing great flying weather, good railroads, unoccupied land and cheap labor, Arizona was a natural location for the United States to build numerous military installations as the country entered World War II in 1941. The U.S. military and the private companies improved the state's economy and they stayed after the war. Tourism began to grow. Increased prosperity and continued migration resulted in a 50% increase in the population from 1940 to 1950.

The Arizona Exposition and State Fair began in 1884 and has been held regularly since 1946. At the State Fair and in local exhibits quilters shared their handiwork over the years. At the 1940 State Fair, Emma Andres won a blue ribbon each for her "Arizona Commemorative" quilt with the state seal and state flag border as well as one for "Out Where the West Begins". At the 1959 Arizona State Fair, Mary Tuttle Pool won a blue ribbon for the "Arizona Map" quilt (p. 6) which is in the DCWM's collection. Goldie Tracy Richmond ran a trading post on the Tohono O'odham Reservation where American Indian-made quilts, baskets and crochet pieces were for sale. Well known for her own beautiful quilts, Goldie regularly won ribbons in the 1960s at the State Fair for her quilts such as "Prospector Quilt" and "Papago Rodeo".

The growth of retirement communities and the Second Quilt Revival of the 20th century contributed to an explosion of quilt making. Quilt guilds such as the Tucson Quilt Guild founded in 1976 and The Arizona Quilt Guild founded in 1978 plus many guilds and community quilt groups promoted quilt exhibits and quilt education.

The study of quilts is a study of our collective history. In the 19th century, album quilts were frequently made as a memento for family and friends

Images left to right: Crazy Quilt with Gold Edge; Four Patch; Arizona Map (details)

departing for the vast frontier or as a commemorative gift for a favorite minister or community leader. Inspired by these album quilts of the past, in 1993 Las Señoras de Socorro Ladies Auxiliary of the Maricopa County Historical Society created the "Wickenburg Album Quilt" (p. 68) which resides in the DCWM's collection. The 25 block patterns depicting landmarks and events of the Wickenburg area are available in the album coloring book for sale in the museum's gift shop.

Arizona quilters mark historical events, patriotism, family blessings and tragedies with quilts. Through quilting, Arizona quilters express their grief at events such as 9/11 and the loss of the 19 Granite Mountain Hotshots in 2013. They provide support and expressions of caring through Quilts of Valor, Project Linus, AZ Blankets for Kids and numerous other charity quilt projects. Quilts are created for fundraising and consciousness-raising such as the national "AIDS Memorial Quilt" project which began in 1987 and the Migrant Quilt Project based in Tucson.

In 1986 inspired by other states' quilt documentation projects, a group of quilters and quilt historians led by Laurene Sinema founded the Arizona Quilt Project. Through a series of Quilt Days held in 26 locations throughout the state the group documented over 3,000 quilts. Additional activities included an educational manual, *Quilt-Ed*, for teachers; a video program, *Arizona Quilts: Pieces of Time*; two exhibitions at University of Arizona's University Art Museum and the Nelson Fine Arts Center on the Arizona State University's Tempe campus; and the publication of *Grand Endeavors: Vintage Quilts and Their Makers*. Large quilt retreats such as Quilt Camp in the Pines, state and local quilt classes and shows as well as special quilt events brought national and international quilt teachers and textile historians who promoted quilt education to the state.

In 1996, the Arizona Quilters Hall of Fame, a virtual museum of Arizona quilts and quilt makers, was incorporated. In September of each year a select group of Arizonans who have significantly contributed to Arizona quilting and quilt history are inducted into the Arizona Quilters Hall of Fame. In the early 2000s, the Arizona Quilt Study Group was established to study quilt history in general and Arizona quilt history in particular. In 2009, the Arizona Centennial Quilt Committee was established and the committee collaborated with the Arizona Historical Society and quilt community volunteers to produce a spectacular "Arizona Centennial Quilt", a line of Centennial fabric, and the Centennial quilt show which was open during 2012 at Arizona Historical Society's Tucson museum.

Shortly after the Centennial quilt activities ended, the Arizona Quilt Documentation Project began under the umbrella of the Arizona Quilters Hall of Fame and the Heritage Quilts Study Group of Sharlot Hall Museum in Prescott. The goal of this project is to pick up where the original state documentation project of the 1980s stopped. With this ongoing project, documentation groups, some affiliated with the Arizona Quilters Hall of Fame, are recording the state's new and antique quilts. These documented quilts are ultimately listed in the *Quilt Index* at Michigan State University. The Desert Caballeros Western Museum's quilts were documented in July 2015 and are currently available on the *Quilt Index* along with over 2,000 other Arizona quilts.

From the 1970s to the present, quilt shops and quilt designers have placed Arizona firmly in the national and international quilt world. (LD and AH)

Image: Wickenburg Album Quilt (detail)

THE QUILTS

ARIZONA MAP QUILT

1954 - 1958
Maker: Mary Pool Tuttle
Cottons, 82" X 92.75"
Donor: Mary Pool Tuttle, Youngtown, Arizona; 92.7

Mary Pool Tuttle won a blue ribbon at the 1959 Arizona State Fair for this fabulous quilt. The hand pieced and hand appliquéd original design tells the story of Arizona. Appliquéd details depict geographic and historical sites such as the State Capitol in Phoenix, Monument Valley, the Casa Grande Monument, the Lowell Observatory in Flagstaff, the Grand Canyon, Mission San Xavier del Bac (also known as the Dove of the Desert), the old Yuma Prison and Montezuma's Castle. The state's major rivers are detailed using black embroidery thread and activities such as fishing, snow skiing and rodeos are represented using appliqué and embroidery. A variety of Arizona plants are shown such as saguaro and organ pipe cacti, a palm tree, a citrus tree and the forests in the northern and eastern parts of the state. Animals shown on the quilt include a coyote, roadrunner, rattlesnake, deer, elk, fish, bear, desert toad, donkey or mule and cattle. Cotton bales, cattle ranching, citrus trees, logging and sheep herding show some of the industries of the state.

Each county in the state is pieced using a different colored fabric and the county seat for each one is indicated using a blue circle. Currently Arizona has 15 counties with the newest county, La Paz, added in 1983 out of parts of Yuma and Mohave counties. Mary's quilt shows the 14 counties in Arizona before La Paz was added. Quilting lines radiate from the state capital and the "border" is cross hatch quilted at six to seven stitches per inch. Beautifully quilted cacti in the border include the saguaro, barrel, organ pipe and prickly pear. The Arizona state flag is beautifully appliquéd in the lower left portion of the quilt.

Born on a farm in Indiana in 1904, Mary came to Arizona in 1936. The amazing details on her quilt clearly show her love of her adopted state and the skill she developed by making over 300 quilts in her lifetime. (AH)

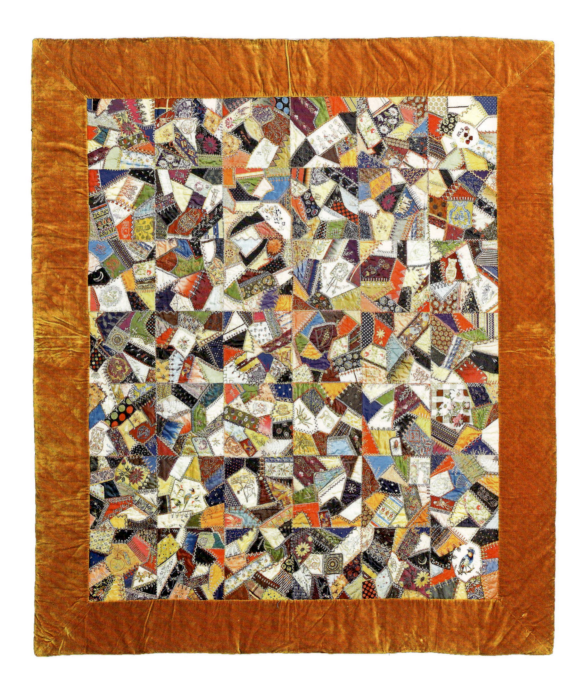

CRAZY QUILT (GOLD EDGE)

1876 - 1900
Maker: Catherine Craig Squier, Overlook Mountain, New York and Rahway, New Jersey
Satin, silk, linen, brocade, 64" X 72.5 "
Donor: Mrs. Catherine S. Stott, Wickenburg; 90.9

This 1884 quilt foundation pieced with satin, silk, velvets and brocades is a wonderful example of the Victorian contained Crazy quilt. The Crazy quilt was a style that fit the heavily decorated Victorian aesthetic. Overlook Mountain in the Hudson River Valley, New York and the date 1884 are prominently embroidered on the quilt. The excellent hand embroidery and lack of shattering of the quilt's silks are some of its many outstanding features.

Fancy embroidery is utilized to depict numerous Japanese fans, vases and cranes. Far Eastern symbols such as the crane, symbol of long life, and the spider web, symbol of prosperity and good luck, are depicted on the quilt and both motifs are commonly found on Crazy quilts from the last quarter of the 19th century.

From the Aesthetic movement, another common motif in the quilt is the owl with spectacles or sayings to stand for wisdom. Also present are many of the motifs found in quilts of this period including Kate Greenaway figures of children, detailed floral embroidery, and decorative ribbons with patches all delicately connected using a virtual catalog of fancy hand embroidery stitches. Tiny figures are stitched inside the small embroidered pitchers and fans and beautiful flowers painted on fabric are included in the quilt. Fancy birds, detailed bugs and tufted spiders are also added. The gold velvet border is in excellent condition and back of the quilt is a silk blend with some shattering. (AH)

CRAZY QUILT (FLORAL LINING)

1876 - 1900
Maker: Mary Boyd Potect, Tennessee, aunt of W. L. Richards
   who owned Brayton's Commercial in Wickenburg
Silk, velvet, 56.5" X 70.5"
Donor: Mrs. Hugh Antrum, Phoenix; 80.1.1

This lovely quilt is another example of the popular contained Crazy quilt. When constructing a contained Crazy quilt, the maker frequently uses a fabric or paper foundation to build a block with oddly shaped fabrics anchoring the fabric pieces with fancy or simple hand or machine stitching. This addition of a foundation plus the heavy fabrics used can make a Crazy quilt very heavy even without a batt. Mary Boyd Potect used silk and velvet with a variety of colored floss stitching to anchor the elements of each of the blocks to the foundation fabric. There are 20 different blocks, each approximately 14 inches square and the quilt is bound with green cording. Similar to other Crazy quilts, this piece has no batt and is tied rather than hand or machine quilted.

There are several hand drawn embroidered butterflies and five embroidered owls on the quilt. Good luck symbols such as the spider web and horseshoe are present as well as fans, teacup, feather, moth or flying bug, cherry branch, a bird on a flowering plant and an anchor. Several embroidered motifs look like hand drawn circles and suns. There are embroidered sunflowers and embroidery of rose buds. There are two intriguing embroidered figures that look like a baseball or cricket player.

Some of the silks are shattering due to the metal salts used to make the silk heavier. Unfortunately this is a common problem that 19th century silks have since there is nothing that can be done to stop or reverse the shattering caused by the metal salts. The back of the quilt is a cotton print. There are no repairs to the quilt. It is a quilt of pleasing arrangement and a lovely catalog of embroidery stitches. (AH)

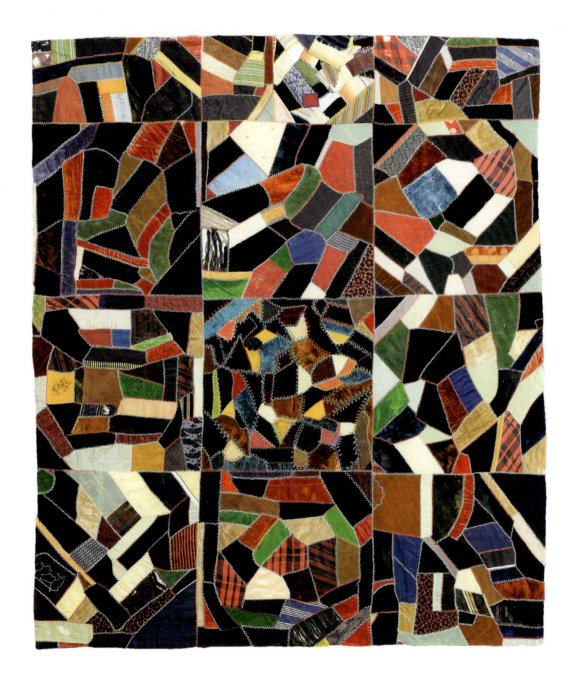

CRAZY QUILT (MAROON/PLUM)

1876 - 1900
Maker: Mary Boyd Potect, Tennessee, aunt of W. L. Richards who owned Brayton's Commercial in Wickenburg
Corduroy, satin, silk, velvet, 64" X 75.5"
Donor: Mrs. Hugh Antrum, Phoenix; 80.1.2

This contained Crazy quilt may be an example of how this quilt style evolved. The Crazy quilt was at its peak in the 1870s to 1880s but as the century came to a close the Crazies generally became less ornate. There are almost none of the motifs similar to the ones in Mary Boyd Potect's other Crazy quilt (p. 10). The embroidered owls, spider webs, horseshoes, and other figures are not found on this quilt. However, it is an excellent catalogue of corduroys and velvets available to women in the last quarter of the 19th century. There are also many other fabrics present – plaids, stripes, solids, florals and dotted. The fabric pieces are still decorated with stitching to attach each piece to a foundation but the stitchery patterns are very plain compared to Mary's other Crazy quilt. Again some of the silks are shattering due to metal salts that have been added to the fabric. There is an ink drawing of a sprig of forget-me-not flowers and an appliqué black velvet rose. One of the blocks contains a lovely black velvet burn-out piece.

The quilt maker used an interesting size and arrangement for the twelve blocks. Nine of the blocks are 21 inches square but the top three blocks are 21 inches by eleven inches. The quilt is tied with off-white cotton thread and the batt is wool. The binding is knife-edge which is constructed by folding the maroon back and top together and anchoring them with almost invisible stitching.

There are questions we might ask about this quilt. Some of the blocks are made out of lots of small scraps; in others the fabric patches are much larger. A few blocks have traditional embellishments such as the inked forget-me-not flowers and the black velvet rose appliqué but most do not. Where these blocks from an exchange? Why is this quilt so different from her other contained Crazy quilt? (AH)

CRAZY QUILT (WINE VELVET)

1876 - 1900
Maker: Unknown
Corduroy, satin, silk, velvet, 63" X 99.5"
Donor: Unknown; 07.12

This elaborate foundation pieced contained Crazy quilt is an excellent example of this genre. The fabrics are in good condition with a minimal amount of disintegration and many of the usual elements of 19th century Crazy quilts are present: fancy stitches in cotton and silk thread, hand embroidered flowers, and good luck and prosperity symbols such as horseshoes with flowers and sheaves of ripe wheat. The 60 blocks measuring 9.5 inches square vary from very well executed to those that are less skillfully done which suggest more than one maker and possibly a Crazy quilt block exchange. The viewer can see the variety of fabric available: brocades, silk moiré, embossed velvets, dress prints and embroidered prints. Many of the fabrics have been selectively cut and there are several very detailed embroideries of rabbits on some of the blocks.

Crazy quilts first became the fashion with upper class women who had the money to purchase expensive fabrics for the home and family plus the leisure time to devote to this intense stitchery. Crazy quilts were meant for show – draped over the piano or settee. Women's magazines published embroidery patterns to use in a Crazy quilt and also published advertisements for silk scraps from mills and factories which made Crazy quilting accessible to quilters with less financial means.

One of the very interesting features of this quilt is the stitching done along the wine velvet border. Different stitch patterns are done in sometimes very bright, almost neon colored floss. There is no batt and the quilt is tied. The back is cotton velvet. (AH)

CRAZY QUILT VARIATION / SQUARE IN A SQUARE

1876-1900
Maker: Unknown
Silk, cottons, satin, velvet, 72" X 72"
Donor: H. K. MacLennan, Wickenburg, a founder of the Desert Caballeros Western Museum; 78.84

Looking at this quilt the first reaction is that it is a Crazy quilt. While incorporating many elements of Crazy quilts, this is actually a traditional format quilt using a block known as "a square in a square". Unlike Crazies that bring many different pieces together in a seemingly random fashion, this quilt is well organized, piecing five squares within one another. Nine major blocks are pieced from a broad range of fabrics and embellished in a manner comparable to Crazies. Bright chenille ribbon is sewn in a zig-zag pattern around the edges of the different blocks. Embroidered motifs in bright floss, appliqués and painted images abound. The colors are daring and practically glowing. Six pieces of coral colored cotton comprise the back. Like a Crazy quilt, this quilt is tied and not quilted.

This is a very unusual quilt. It exhibits elements that suggest a Southwest influence. The bright pinks, turquoises and golds are similar to the colors in native costumes, piñatas and the bright crepe paper flowers used in Mexican celebrations. Images that appear to be Native American katsinas and the mariposa flower, native to the desert, are placed throughout the quilt. Even figures that resemble milagros – the silver folk art charms popular in Mexican culture and used as a votive offering – can be identified. Hearts with hands, a dove of peace and what looks like a rosary surrounding a heart are skillfully embroidered.

The one thing that this quilt does share with traditional Crazy quilts is extensive deterioration. Nearly every piece of fabric is damaged or disintegrating. The chenille ribbons are falling apart and the embroidery is breaking away. It seems to shatter at the slightest touch. This is unfortunate because there is no doubt that this is truly a one of a kind quilt. (LD)

CROWN OF THORNS

1850 - 1875
Maker: Lois Dickson, wife of a Texas state legislator
Cottons, 80" x 81"
Donor: Mr. and Mrs. William Blanchet; 80.31

Contemporary quilt makers may know this pattern as "New York Beauty". It is a powerfully graphic design that is difficult to piece. Though suffering fading and fabric loss in the greens, the bold use of red and green make this quilt an eye popper. Constructing the pattern was not easy. Hand pieced, the hundreds of "sawtooth" pieces with their spikey points create an image of piercing thorns.

What is especially appealing about this particular quilt is the inclusion of the four small star or sunburst blocks in the center of each "crown". This is an unusual touch as most quilts of this pattern use solid blocks in those areas. These have the same spikey element but on a much smaller scale. Piecing these was not an easy task. Many modern quilters rely on a method known as "paper piecing" which involves utilizing a paper foundation to achieve sharp and precise points. Doing it all by hand was no easy task.

The quilting is done by hand in an outline and echo format. It is closely done with approximately a quarter of an inch between quilting lines. This dense quilting is most likely what has kept the deteriorating green from total disintegration. This is an excellent example of why quilts should not be washed frequently. Hard scrubbing, agitation, hot water and the weight of the quilt when wet all contributed to the rapid deterioration of this graphic dazzler. The binding is not original and was probably added sometime in the 20th century. (LD)

DRUNKARD'S PATH

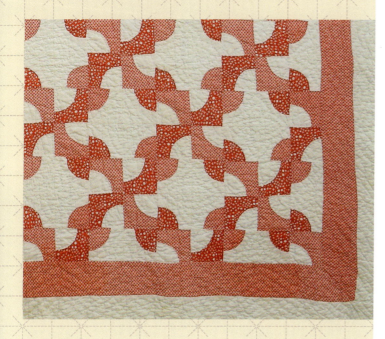

1901 - 1929
Maker: Janet Wright (?)
Cottons, 76" by 88"
Donor: Mrs. John Sexson; 86.32.6

Quilts with this pattern are typically made using just two fabrics such as red and white or blue and white. The contrasting reds in this quilt give an interesting interpretation of a traditional pattern. Clearly the quilt maker had a more playful and subtle vision of this traditional pattern and one might speculate about her deliberate choices in designing her quilt.

The quilt is all cotton with a lovely scalloped border and strong graphic appeal. The quilt is densely hand quilted with large stitches – three to four stitches per inch – using an off-white cotton thread. The quilting outlines the patches and "V" shaped parallel lines and echo quilting is used on the scalloped border.

A common myth about this pattern is that there is a connection to the Women's Christian Temperance Union (W.C.T.U.) but currently there is no known documented proof. It is true that many "Drunkard's Path" quilts are made using the two colors of the W.C.T.U. – white for purity and blue for water (water being the purest drink).

There are 672 blocks measuring 2-5/8" square. The batt is cotton and there is some damage to the quilt including small tears or holes and wear to the binding. No repairs were discerned.

Other names for this pattern include "Wonder of the World" (*Farm and Fireside*, 1884), "Wanderer's Path in the Wilderness" (*Farm and Home*, 1888) and "Double Wrench" (*Ohio Farmer*, 1889). The pattern was also printed in *Woman's World* in 1931 and called "Solomon's Puzzle".

There is a single name written on the back of this quilt with a laundry pen: Janet Wright. Was she the maker? (AH)

EMBROIDERED RED WORK SUMMER SPREAD

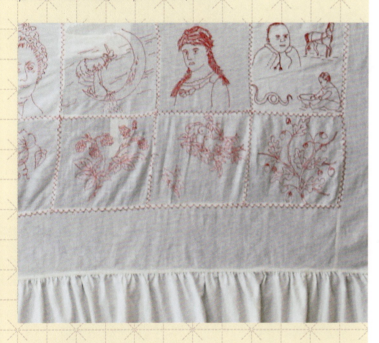

1876 - 1900
Maker: Ida Rand Harmon, Iowa Falls, Hardin County, Iowa
Cotton, red embroidery floss, 88" X 84"
Donor: Mrs. E. J. Foley, Wickenburg; 87.48.5

This summer spread has been lovingly repaired over the years. It is a wonderful sampler of red colored blocks including pictures of George and Martha Washington. Red work embroidery used a deep Turkey red embroidery thread and peaked in popularity around 1900. The patterns on this spread and many others were initially used to decorate household items such as tea towels, napkins, pillows and children's clothing. The large center floral embroidery may have been a design for a pillow top or back splash over the kitchen sink.

Available beginning in the 1880s, red work patterns ranged from simple to very complex. Pre-printed blocks were sold for a nominal amount – one penny – and these little blocks became known as penny squares. Around 1900 red work blocks were used in bed quilts and sometimes a summer spread such as this lovely example.

The spread is nicely embroidered on a very thin background fabric with common motifs of the era such as owls, animals, florals, a Victorian lady and possibly a picture of Marie Curie. The maker also combined several usual red work motifs in a single block. While blocks are hand embroidered they are machine-pieced together.

Machine-applied eleven inch ruffles at the top and bottom of the piece gives this summer spread an interesting configuration. The original acquisition document indicated there were ruffles on three sides of this spread. There is no information about what became of the third ruffle if indeed there were three. Some of the repairs are done including reverse appliqué, machine darning and an iron-on patch in one place. (AH)

EMBROIDERED TOP

1901 - 1929
Maker: Ida Rand Harmon, Iowa Falls, Iowa
Cottons, 82.5"X 73.75"
Donor: Mrs. E. J. Foley, Wickenburg; 87.48.4

This multi-colored embroidered top is a wonderful sampler of embroidery patterns available in newspapers and magazines. Ruby Short McKim published many embroidered quilt patterns as well as appliqué and pieced patterns. "Bird Life" or "Audubon" quilt by Ruby Short McKim was published in the *Kansas City Star* in 1928 and included 24 different bird patterns. Many newspapers published a pattern weekly for readers to cut out or trace. For a fee readers could also send away for the patterns. Church bulletins often had Bible themed embroidery patterns which could be delivered by mail. During this time designers were known to ignore copyrights – multiple pattern designers could have one or more of their designs in this piece.

One of the interesting features of this coverlet is that Ida Rand Harmon embroidered traditional red work blocks such as the owls in multi-colored floss rather than the usual Turkey red. As traditional red work decreased in popularity, designers encouraged quilters to use multiple colors in their embroidered blocks. The Rainbow Block Company in Ohio printed blocks with colored ink giving the quilt maker color suggestions. These blocks became very popular and other companies began to imitate this innovation.

The motifs in the coverlet included flowers such as tiger lilies, lily of the valley, tulips, trumpet flowers, lavender, blue bells, water lilies and carnations There are many animals represented such as plow horses, mischievous cats, owls, a puppy, a mare and her foal, hunting dogs, plus the bird blocks from "Bird Life". Children are shown playing with a pet, picking flowers and playing dress up as bride and groom. These 72 different nine inch square blocks are machine pieced together to make the coverlet. (AH)

FLORAL BOUQUET

1901 - 1929
Maker: Helen Davis Rothermel (1882-1971), Reading, Pennsylvania
Cottons, 51" X 83.75"
Donor: Mrs. Fritz Rothermel; 86.4.1

Since the color and design of this quilt are typical of kit quilts of this era, this quilt is probably a lovely example of a well-loved Floral Appliqué kit quilt. The colors of the quilt are soft and the fabrics are worn, giving a sense of softness and gentleness. The family dates the quilt as having been made in 1915 which also fits the style of the quilt.

As early as 1898, The Ladies Art Company sold kit quilt blocks and finished quilts. In 1908 the Wilkinson Quilt Company began as a cottage industry and grew to become incorporated in 1914. Ona and Rosa Wilkinson of Ligonier, Indiana sold their quilt kits and finished quilts by mail order, in specialty shops and at resorts. The success of and demand for kit quilts inspired other quilt designers such as Marie Webster, Ann Orr and Mary McElwain to form quilt companies which sold patterns, blocks, quilt tops and completed quilts.

The colors of the quilt also suggest it is a kit quilt – the pink, blue, Nile green, and lavender – as does the floral bouquet center medallion design with a floral frame which incorporates flowers from the bouquet. The bouquet has pink roses, pink tulips, blue forget-me-nots, bluebells and lavender violets all tied together with a lavender bow.

The floral designs are hand appliquéd and the quilt is hand quilted with off-white thread at eight stitches per inch. The quilting patterns used include cross hatch, feathering, floral and wreaths. The back of the quilt is a gold cotton fabric. Helen Davis Rothermel's quilt delights the viewer's eye with the beautiful colors, design, appliqué and quilting. This quilt makes it easy to see why kit quilts are still popular in the 21st century. (AH)

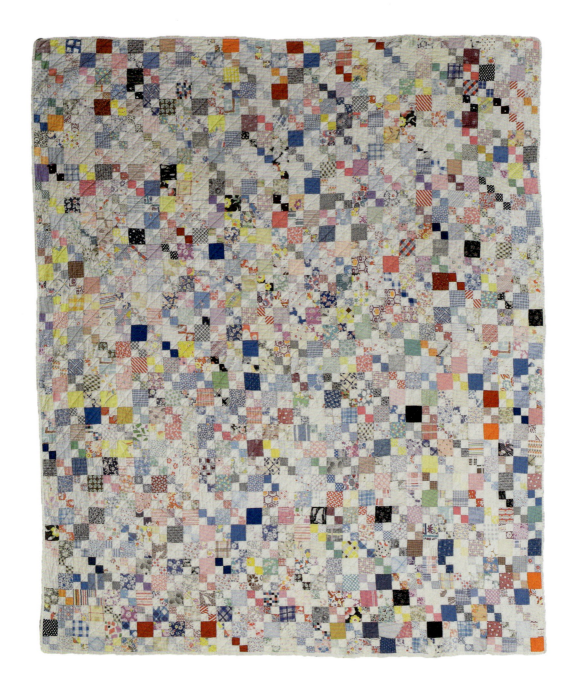

FOUR PATCH

1930 - 1949
Maker: Unknown
Cottons, 66" X 77.5 "
Donor: Unknown; 4.07

The humble "Four Patch" shines in this quilt. It is a simple block to construct but pieced with alternating solids and prints it yields a pleasing design. This patch was one of the first blocks a young girl in the 19th century would learn to piece. Perhaps the young lady would use her "Four Patch" blocks to make a little quilt for a doll.

Interestingly the blocks are hand pieced. Possibly the maker hand pieced the blocks as she spent time in a waiting room, watched children at play or while she listened to the radio in the evening. The variety of fabrics used in this piece is impressive – solids, florals, geometrics, novelties, conversation prints, stripes, shirtings, plaids, checks, paisleys, feed sack style and mourning prints – which hints that the quilt maker dug deep into her scrap bag for her pieces.

It is hand quilted at five stitches per inch and the distance between quilting lines is 1.5 inches. The batt is cotton and has shifted over time. (AH)

GOOSE IN THE POND

1876 - 1900
Maker: Unknown
Cottons, 57.5"X 79"
Donor: Unknown; 82.1

Little is known about this quilt but the fabrics and how it was made give hints about its history. The fabrics in the blocks include solids and prints such as florals, geometrics, paisleys and plaids. The presence of mourning prints and chambray plus the quilt style suggest this quilt was made in the last quarter of the 19th century. The top of the quilt is hand and machine pieced.

There are twelve blocks that are about 15 inches square. This is another block with multiple names such as "Young Man's Fancy" (*Modern Priscilla*); "Geometric Garden" (*Grandma Dexter*), and "Scrap Bag" (if the shading is reversed) (*Kansas City Star*, 1935).

The sashing is the same color as the background fabric in the blocks. The cornerstones are blue five inch squares. The batt is cotton and the quilt is tied suggesting the quilt may have been needed in a hurry. It is also possible the maker just preferred to tie quilts, particularly those that would be used heavily as this one was. The back is muslin which has yellowed slightly over time. (AH)

HEART QUILT

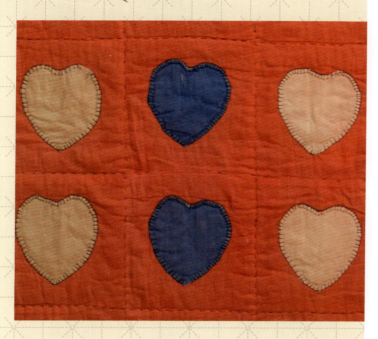

1901 - 1929
Maker: mother of Homer G. Alexander
Solid cottons, 63" X 74"
Donor: Mrs. Ann Alexander, Wickenburg, daughter-in-law of maker; 87.11

While the fabrics of this quilt are limited and plain, the maker has used her resources effectively to create a pleasing design. The Nile green hearts are on the far left and right of the quilt while the other heart columns alternate tan/pink and blue on the red background. Blue and green hearts "glow" off the red block fabric. It is possible that some of the fabrics were hand dyed, particularly the pink which has started to become tan.

The wear on the quilt indicates it was loved and heavily used. There is damage to the quilt – discoloration, shrinkage of some fabric, fading, tears and holes. Repairs to the quilt include tears and holes sewn together and a replaced floral binding on the top and bottom of the quilt probably in the 1950s. The family's date for this quilt is 1900.

There are 56 buttonhole hand appliquéd heart blocks each on a nine inch square. At first the embroidery floss used to appliqué the hearts looks black but it is actually a very dark brown. The quilt was machine pieced and hand quilted at two stitches per inch. The batt is wool and the back is the same red cotton as the background on the front.

While this quilt is not a great beauty, it must have been a beautiful memento for Homer Alexander since he kept it with him when he moved to Arizona in 1965 after working 36 years for General Motors in Detroit, Michigan. (AH)

HEN AND CHICKS/DUCKS AND DUCKLINGS

1876 - 1900
Maker: Mrs. David Jones, wife of mining superintendent at Congress-Octave Mine
Cottons, 71" X 82.5"
Donor: Mary Jones, Wickenburg; 75.20.1

This is a heavy quilt both in weight and color. Made up of thousands of various size triangles this quilt displays a broad collection of late 19th century indigos, mourning prints and purples representing hens surrounded by flocks of little chicks.

Constructed mostly of traditional cotton, one of the fabrics used is cretonne (CREE-tawn or cruh-TAWN), a rather coarsely woven, heavy cotton fabric that was generally used in draperies and slipcovers. Though colorfully printed, the dye had a tendency to run as is exhibited in this quilt. The dye in the patches of large scale, pinkish florals is plainly leaching into surrounding fabrics. This was probably because the quilt either got wet or was washed at some point.

By the end of the 19th century, when this quilt was made, cretonne was considered a cheap fabric, too coarse for patchwork. Its rather cluttered pattern also made it less desirable, especially as fashion was turning away from the overly ornate Victorian aesthetic to a simpler, more low-keyed approach. It may be that the maker had access to an upholstery shop or a dry goods store (Brayton's Commercial?) and simply made use of what was at hand, proving once again that quilters are a thrifty lot. (LD)

JACKSON STAR

1950 – 1975
Maker: Unknown
Cottons, 66.75" X 80"
Donor: Unknown, not accessioned

Little is known about this quilt yet the fabrics used and the quilting give hints to when it was made. The fabrics used in this quilt are solids, polka dots, floral, novelty, paisleys and plaid, checked and feed sack type. One of the fabrics is a white with hot pink prints of kitchen items such as forks, spoons, plates, knives, cups, aprons and goblets. The white fabric printed with green olives was originally a pre-printed pattern for what seems to be a halter top and shorts or play skirt. Pieces of the fabric with the printed instructions for making the clothing are used in several of the star blocks. One can see partial directions such as "narrow hems along… halter…along remaining seam… put on and tie…and waist". The 20 star blocks are hand and machine pieced.

The block pattern "Jackson Star" was published in The *Kansas City Star* May 16, 1931. There are other very similar star blocks which have the same piecing but each maker's fabric selection for the pieces gives a different look. These similar patterns include "Old Maid's Patience" (*Nancy Cabot*, June 24, 1933) and "Maple Leaf" (*Capper's*, October 24, 1933). Many patterns have multiple names depending on the publisher and they were frequently renamed for the publication's particular theme. The blocks are set with green sashing and there are three inch square yellow cornerstones. Typical of quilts of this era the back is plain muslin. The quilt has a cotton batt and is machine quilted using single parallel lines with a white poly wrapped thread. (AH)

LEMOYNE STAR (CARMAN)

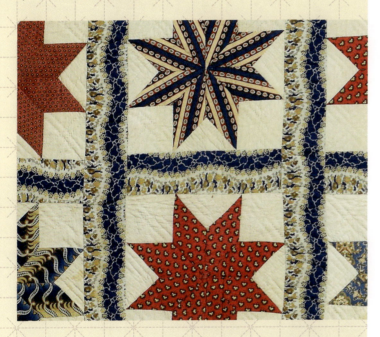

1850 - 1875
Maker: Fanny Lobbins Carman (1828-1905), Long Island, New York
Cottons, 84" x 102"
Donor: Mrs. Carolyn Modeen, Sun City, Arizona, from the estate of Florence M. Tannaker; 94.8.2

One of the oldest quilts in the collection, this stunning eight point "Lemoyne Star" quilt is the work of a master quilter. In the lower left corner is the ink signature of Fanny Carman. Fanny's skilled hands and eye made remarkable use of a broad range of early 19th century fabrics. Being near the fabric mills of New England and near port cities made it easy for Fanny to obtain so many different fabrics. Block and roller prints of chintz, ombre, Turkey reds, madders and Prussian blue form the 30 stars which are separated by a serpentine patterned sashing.

Reminiscent of the "stack and whack" method used by today's quilters, Fanny selectively cut her fabric to display specific images and patterns. Many of the stars produce an almost kaleidoscopic effect. This was a "wasteful" process and indicates Fanny had the funds to purchase enough fabric to use just the areas of the pattern she wanted.

In near pristine condition this quilt may have been a "best" quilt and was never washed as two of the chintz stars still retain their glazing. The quilting is done in an outline pattern, typical for scrappy quilts of the period and the thin wool batting allowed for close quilting stitches. Fanny had an excellent graphic instinct as the sharp contrast between the Prussian blue of the sashing, the bold colors of the stars and the stark white background cause the viewer's eye to dance across the quilt. Fanny may have made her quilt for a specific bed as there are borders on only the right side and the bottom of the quilt suggesting the bed may have been against a wall with pillows at the top. (LD)

LEMOYNE STAR (FREED)

1876 - 1900
Maker: Mary Anne Freed (b.1838), Iowa
Cottons, 81" x 91.5"
Donor: Joyce Freed LaFon; 86.5

Here is a quilt that employs an unlikely combination of colors yet produces a pleasing and vivid effect. Double pink and overdyed green Lemoyne Stars rest in a chrome yellow bed divided by madder red sashing and surrounded by a Lancaster blue border. These colors were often the choice of Pennsylvania German quilters. Mary Anne Freed was a German immigrant.

This is a large quilt with large components. The sashing and cornerstones are oversized as is the border. The quilt may have been made for a specific bed as the top border is narrower than the sides and bottom. The copper red sashing was cut with an eye to pattern making sure the white figures in the print are in the proper horizontal or vertical placement.

The quilt is entirely hand pieced and quilted at five stitches to the inch. The batting is a thin cotton allowing the quilt to drape nicely. Although it has suffered some fabric loss over the years and is a bit stained it is a lovely quilt that still appeals. (LD)

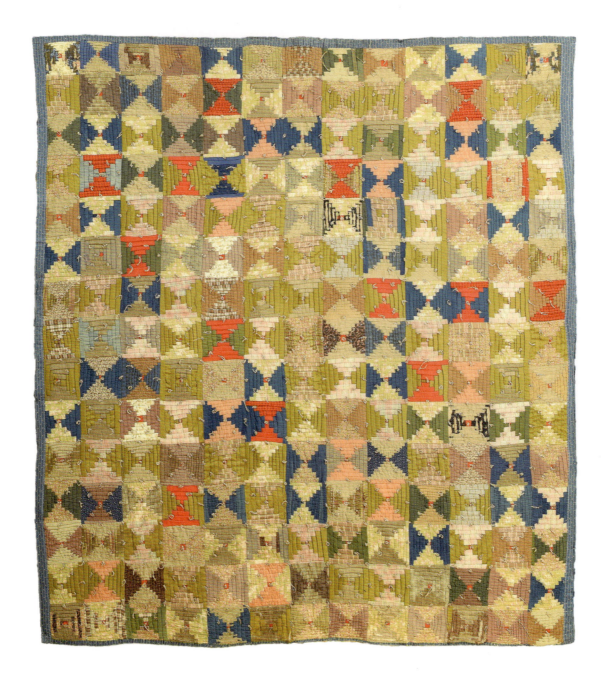

LOG CABIN – COURTHOUSE STEPS

1876 - 1900
Maker: Unknown
Cottons, wool challis, 67.5" x 74.5"
Donor: Unknown; 1.17

"Courthouse Steps" is a popular variation of the Log Cabin block, one of the most familiar of all quilt blocks. Besides the lively graphic designs achieved by varying the placement of the blocks, quilters are drawn to the Log Cabin by its easy construction, making it a favorite of beginning and less skilled quilters. Additionally, it uses scraps of all sorts, including some of the smallest pieces. It is not unusual to find many of the "logs" in a block stitched together from two or more pieces of fabric. And it doesn't rely on using a single kind of fabric. Many a Log Cabin quilt combines cotton, wool, twill, corduroy, silk and velvet all in one quilt. This quilt is constructed using primarily cottons and wool challis.

This is another quilt that demands a second look. Close inspection reveals that it is a "time-span" quilt – i.e. a quilt that was started by one generation and finished years later by another. The quilt is constructed by hand and the blocks are foundation pieced to squares of beautiful late 19th century cotton prints. Many are pieced onto a square of resist printed indigo. The construction is relatively well done.

Many Log Cabin quilts would simply end at this point and add a binding. On this quilt a second person has added a thin wool batting and a poorly applied cotton backing. Instead of separate binding, the second maker brought the backing fabric forward in a haphazard and inconsistent manner. Many Log Cabins that do have batting and backing are generally quilted in the ditch or straight through a log. This quilt is tied. The result is a somewhat heavy quilt. Perhaps the maker needed a quilt for warmth and protection and finished the quilt as simply and as quickly as she could. (LD)

LOG CABIN – STRAIGHT FURROWS

1901 - 1929
Maker: Annie Pratt Perrine, Freehold, New Jersey
Silk, satin, velvet, 64" X 64"
Donor: Margaret B. Darby, Wickenburg, maker's great niece; 90.30

This quilt is a cousin to the elaborate Crazy quilts of the 19th century. It incorporates many of the same fabrics and, like them, was meant for display rather than warmth. Unlike the highly decorated Victorian pieces this quilt is simpler and much less fussy which some viewers may find more appealing.

The maker had an excellent sense of design and color. The strong contrast between lights and darks in the furrows provides a bold background for the central diamond. Each block sports a velvet center. The border is composed of long, pointed, brightly colored silk strips which form fan-like corners. The overall effect is energetic and almost Art Deco in appearance.

Once again, close inspection reveals a secret past. Most silk or Crazy quilts were not meant for a bed or covering. They were display pieces made to show off the maker's needle skills and good taste and intended to be draped across a piano or table. This quilt was machine sewn. A tiny chain stitch holds the silks and satin logs to a muslin foundation and also attaches the foundation pieced border. This was where the maker intended her work to end. But look closely and there is evidence someone had other plans. Tufts of wool and bits of gold floss at the corner of each block show that the quilt at one time had a back, batting and was tied. The border has remnants of white floss. When the backing was added and when it was removed remains a mystery. Happily none of the "updating" has caused much damage to an otherwise stunning and delightful quilt. (LD)

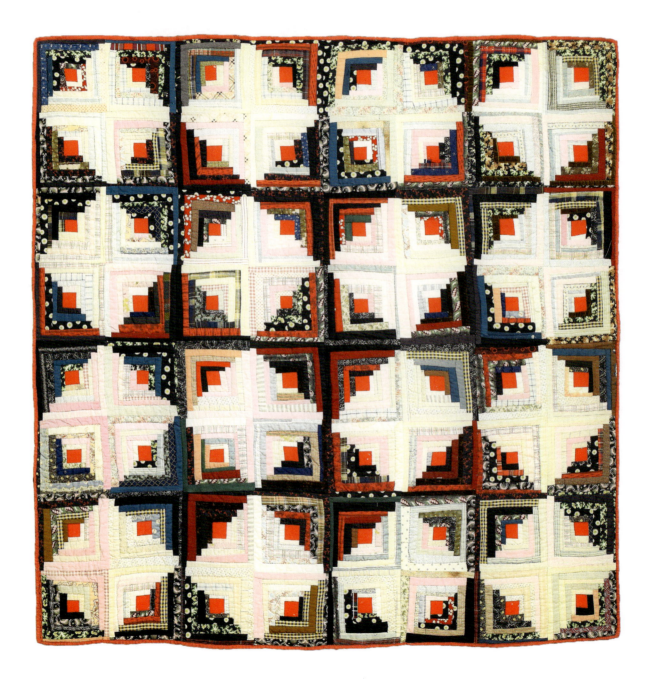

LOG CABIN – SUNSHINE AND SHADOW/DIAMONDS

1876 - 1900
Maker: Rex family, Slatingham, Pennsylvania
Flannels, wool challis, cottons, corduroy, 67.5" x 67.5"
Donor: Mae Roberts, originally from Easton, Pennsylvania, died in Wickenburg in 2001; 75.443

A typical example of the era, this late 19th century quilt is a contrast in lights and darks. The Log Cabin pattern was popular throughout the last half of the 19th century and continues to be a favorite today. It makes use of all sorts of fabric scraps and the quick and easy piecing make it a perfect pattern for the beginning quilter.

The block resembles the construction of a log cabin with "logs" of fabric applied concentrically around a center square, usually red, that is said to represent the hearth of the cabin. Quilt makers employed a variety of settings. This one is placed in a diamond pattern with the fabric logs of wool challis, flannels, cottons, shirtings, corduroy and velvets surrounding red wool "hearths". With each block foundation pieced to a cotton square the maker may have been in a hurry to complete the quilt as the fabric logs are of random sizes and the final block is not always straight or square. This casual approach to size and consistency may set contemporary quilters' teeth on edge but it was obviously not that important to the maker and adds to the overall rustic charm.

Like most Log Cabin quilts the maker used a wide variety of fabrics, colors and prints. A surprising addition is the extensive use of "brights" – those circa 1890 fabrics that incorporate bright, garish colors that a flower child of the 1960s would identify as "dayglow". Unlike many foundation pieced Log Cabins that are tied, this quilt is quilted in the ditch. (LD)

LOST SHIPS

1876 - 1900
Maker: Unknown
Cottons, 87.5" x 88"
Donor: Peg Bowman Darby, former Desert Caballeros
 Western Museum curator; 93.23

The maker of this colorful quilt had a strong sense of graphic design. Bright red half square triangles paired with white ground shirting sail in a sea of smaller multi-colored half square triangles. The maker created an unusual pattern by framing each large block with a row of small scrappy half square blocks giving the illusion of sashing. At each corner she used red and cheddar fabric to create eye popping cornerstones.

The quilt is a virtual catalog of late 19th century fabric. Mourning prints, Hershey browns, clarets, plaids, shirtings and double pinks spill across the quilt. Older fabrics of indigo and copper madders add to the powerful use of contrasting colors.

The quilt is both machine and hand pieced. With a thin cotton batting it is quilted in an overall cross hatch pattern and done with a fine hand. The quilting measures six stitches to the inch. The double pink binding is machine applied.

This quilt is a bold statement of a maker who loved color and energy. The eye dances over the rows of ships as they sail in a storm of fabric. (LD)

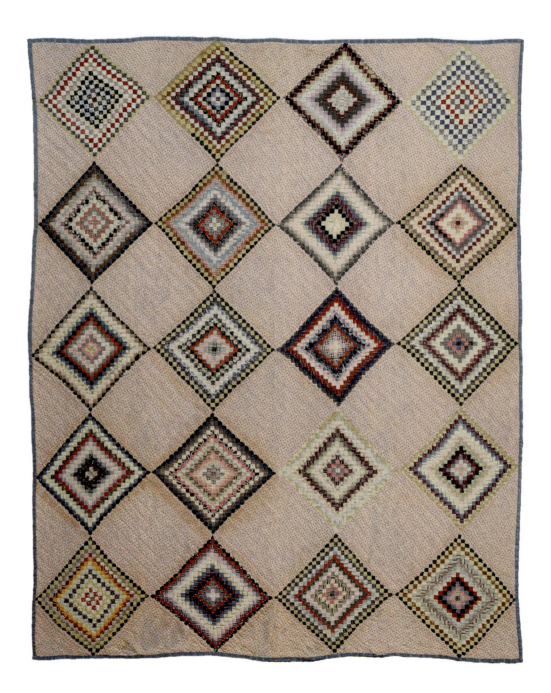

MANY TRIPS AROUND THE WORLD

1876 - 1900
Maker: Lula Maude Cochran Good, Lacey, Iowa
Cottons, 62.5" X 72.5"
Donor: Margaret Wigglesworth, Lehigh Acres, Florida; 92.24

Made up of hundreds of tiny squares measuring less than an inch in width this delightful quilt is a true catalog of 19th century fabrics. The pattern is also known as "Boston Pavement" or "Boston Commons". The eye is dazzled as the minute squares march around each other in what seems an endless parade. The blocks are hand pieced and the quilt is machine assembled. The batting is cotton and the quilt is hand quilted at six stitches to the inch in an overall double rod pattern.

This quilt took quite a while to assemble beginning with the mind boggling task of cutting each tiny square by hand. But once the pieces were cut it was no doubt pleasant hand work as the maker could do it while relaxing at home or visiting with friends and family. Often piecework like this was chosen because of its portability thus allowing the maker to carry it with her if she was away from home.

The pattern is also a thrifty choice because it uses scraps of all sizes, colors and prints. Not only could the maker use every tiny bit from her scrap bag but she could request the smallest of scraps from others. All she basically needed was light and dark fabric.

Although the quilt suffers from age it is still an appealing piece. (LD)

MULTI-COLORED SILK TRIANGLE QUILT

1901 - 1929
Maker: Unknown
Silks, rayon, cottons, 70" by 74"
Donor: Mrs. John Sexson; 86.32.5

This quilt would certainly fit in the Modern Quilt Movement of the 21st century even though it was made a hundred years earlier. The blocks are elongated half square triangles made of striped silks, rayons and cottons. The stripes in the fabric suggest the pieces came from shirts and dresses in the early decades of the 20th century. To obtain such a variety of striped fabric, perhaps the maker ordered mill ends through the post or was or knew a dressmaker.

The piecing and placing of the triangles provides a wild and strong visual impact. Intrigued, the viewer is drawn in to look closely at the pieces. The sizes of the half-square triangles vary suggesting the maker used some free form machine piecing technique.

There is some chain stitch embroidery and traces of embroidery that has been removed. The back is a cotton flannel and the quilt is machine quilted with no batt in single parallel lines. (AH)

NINE PATCH

1930 - 1949
Maker: Ida Rand Harmon (1856-1950), Iowa Falls, Hardin County, Iowa
Cottons, 76" x 91"
Donor: Mrs. E. J. Foley, Wickenburg, maker's granddaughter; 87.48.3

This is an unusual quilt and a prime example of quilters never throwing out any fabrics. Upon first glance the viewer sees a center of hundreds of small nine patch blocks framed by two borders and a wide binding. Close inspection reveals that something is a bit different about this quilt. The fabrics in the borders and the main body of the quilt are not from the same era and are, in fact, from two different centuries! The center was most likely made in the last part of the 19th century although it does contain fabric from earlier decades. The border is comprised of fabric from the late 1930s/early 1940s. The backing is the same as the binding fabric and the entire piece has been rather quickly machine quilted. Historians date quilts by the latest fabrics and though the center of the quilt is circa 1880s, because of the borders and the backing the quilt would be identified as circa 1940.

The completion of this piece crossed several decades and multiple generations. Not an uncommon practice, some quilters refer to this as a "time-span" quilt. The question is who did what? Is this a piece started by a mother and finished by a daughter? Did the quilter make the center as a young woman and complete it as an old lady? Whatever its history it is apparent that the top was valued enough to have been completed and put to use. (LD)

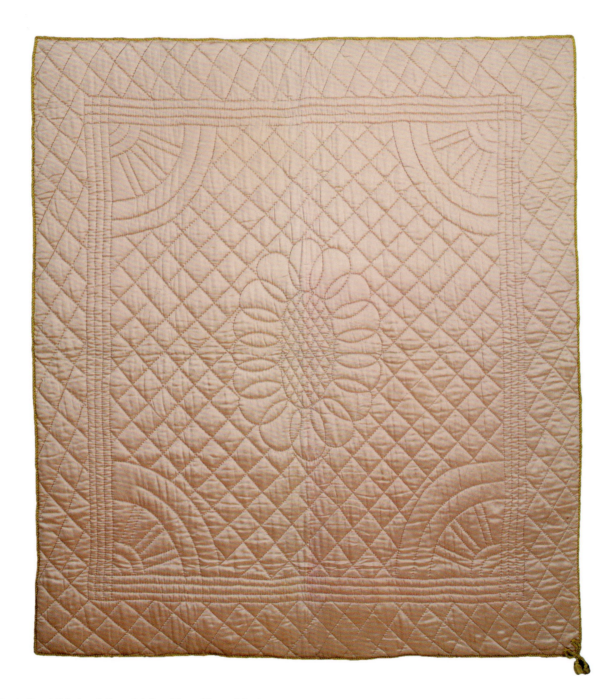

PINK SATIN WHOLE CLOTH

1930 - 1949
Maker: Unknown
Satin, 71" x 76.5"
Donor: Margaret Metcalf; 78.470

This shiny comforter was a popular style of bed covering throughout much of the 20th century. Made both commercially and at home they added glamour to many a bedroom. This is a two sided quilt. Pink on one side and gold on the other it allowed the owner to change her décor as she pleased. Well-constructed, this quilt still displays the pencil lines used to mark the quilting designs. Quilted in a central medallion format, there are fans at the corners and the body of the quilt is covered in a cross-hatch design. A thick wool batting gives dimension to the quilting as well as providing warmth. Setting it off, the maker added gold cording in lieu of binding that ends in a whimsical bow at the bottom corner.

This quilt may be the product of a cottage industry. Many women designed and produced quilts for sale as a way of earning money to help a family get by financially. Both country and city dwellers did piece work for pay. Most women worked at home. Although many home quilters produced the entire quilt, commercial businesses often used an assembly line format – hiring one woman to piece the quilt, another to quilt it and yet another to sew the binding. Many quilters supplemented their income by hand quilting tops for others. There is no tag or marking on the quilt so we cannot say definitively how and why this quilt was made. It could have been made for sale or it could be the work of an excellent and tasteful home quilter. (LD)

POINSETTIA APPLIQUÉ TOP

1876 - 1900
Maker: Unknown
Cottons, 96" x 96.5"
Donor: Unknown; 86.42.6

Nine appliqué blocks set on point are reminiscent of the striking red and green appliqué quilts of the mid-19th century. By the late 1800s this style was no longer in fashion. Although this top does not exhibit the skill and mastery of the earlier quilts it nevertheless has a primitive charm which delights the eye.

The swirling flowers appear to be poinsettias with berries and leaves flowing outward from the blossoms. Like earlier quilts this top uses only red and green fabrics accented with a bold cheddar. However, a tell-tale sign that this is a late 19th century quilt is the loss of color in some of the greens and reds. This is brought on by the fugitive properties of certain chemical dyes and accounts for the large number of red and tan (initially red and green) quilts of the late 1800s.

This appliquéd top is the product of an enthusiastic but not exceptionally skilled maker. The appliqué pieces are not smoothly turned and size and placement of the flowers is inconsistent. For some reason only the red berries are stuffed. The top is machine assembled and unfortunately does not lie flat. This may be the reason it was never quilted. (LD)

RED AND GREEN APPLIQUÉ SUMMER SPREAD

1850 - 1875
Maker: Eliza Jane McMillen (1818-1903), Erie County, New York
Cottons, 72" X 88"
Donor: Mrs. E. J. Foley, Wickenburg; 87.48.6

This summer spread has ten full blocks on point with green sashing and nine half blocks with two quarter blocks. The motifs are appliquéd with white thread and the design of the blocks is probably original or based on a quilt previously seen by the maker. The blocks are hand pieced and hand appliquéd. The green is an over-dye and the red is the popular Turkey red of this time period. An over-dye green fabric is made by either dyeing blue over yellow or yellow over blue to make green since until the last quarter of the 19th century there was no one step green dye.

Red and green appliqué quilts were very popular in the mid 19thcentury partly because that color combination is so common in nature, is pleasing to the eye, and Turkey red was a stable color. Additionally women's magazines such as *Godey's* published needlework designs of all types so women with access to such publications could see the latest trends. Using red and green with accent colors such as chrome orange, chrome yellow and blue was popular in the eastern and Midwestern parts of the country and as the population moved further west this quilt style came with women pioneers as completed quilts and design ideas.

The binding on the spread is hand sewn and the half and quarter blocks have a lovely green vine with red buds which give an appliquéd border effect. One repair is possibly from the 19th century and others are more recent. (AH)

SAWTOOTH

1876 - 1900
Maker: Unknown
Cottons, 73" X 74"
Donor: Unknown; 75.20.2

This quilt would have been quite a stunner in its day. Unfortunately it was well loved and much of the fabric is either lost or disintegrating, especially the blacks.

The quilt contains a variety of colors and prints, and with the exception of the white points of the stars, the maker didn't seem too concerned about consistency of fabric choice and placement. However, the strong contrast between the bold coppery print in the spacer blocks and the blacks, blues, greens and reds of the stars creates an appealing graphic quality. Today's quilt maker might find this approach rather haphazard but for the quilters of yesteryear this didn't appear to be an issue. Though fabric was certainly plentiful and affordable a quilter may not have been able to purchase enough to follow a specific color scheme. Or she may have been in a bit of a hurry and simply used whatever was in the scrap bag. Or she just may not have cared about using only certain fabrics.

A thin cotton batting and simple double rod quilting across the body of the quilt allowed the quilt maker to complete the quilt with relative speed. (LD)

SOUTHERN BELLE

1930 - 1949
Maker: Unknown
Cottons, 76.5"X 80"
Donor: Mrs. Paul Pfingstag; 76.307

The pattern for this sweet and lovely quilt is "Sunbonnet Lady" or "Southern Belle". There are many variations and names of this pattern including "Colonial Lady", "Umbrella Lady" and "Old Fashioned Lady". These patterns were published by newspapers such as the *Kansas City Star* and *Chicago Tribune* and magazines like *Needlecraft, The Workbasket, Grandma Dexter* and *Aunt Martha*. Regardless of the name of the pattern some quilt historians trace the evolution of this pattern back to Kate Greenaway's *Sunbonnet Babies*. Now this pattern and its variations are available in books, individual patterns and free on some internet pattern web sites.

There are 28 blocks measuring 10.5 inches square. The colors on this quilt are strong and clear. The maker did an excellent job pairing her prints and solids for the lady's dress and coordinating umbrella. Her hand appliqué stitches are almost invisible and the embroidered details are finely executed. The cotton fabrics used in this quilt include plaids, florals, paisleys, geometrics and possibly feed sack prints. The flowers in each block are accented with black French knots and the stems and leaves are embroidered with green floss. The blocks are machine pieced together and delightful blue stars cover the block intersections.

Partial stars are also used in the border area of the quilt. The maker's use of the blue stars adds an extra sparkle to the piece. The alternate blocks are quilted in feathered wreaths and the stars are emphasized through a large star quilt motif. The appliqué pieces are outline quilted. Quilting at eight stitches per inch, the maker was very good at her art. The batt is cotton and while there is some fading the quilt is in good condition and is a wonderful example of this quilt pattern. (AH)

WHITE WORK/ CANDLEWICK SUMMER SPREAD

1854
Maker: Maria Estey Dickson, Piqua, Ohio
Cottons, 89.75" x 78"
Donor: Mrs. Raymond Good, maker's granddaughter; 92.15.1

This beautiful white work coverlet is in an extremely fragile state and is very nearly in pieces. In spite of early repairs the fabric has disintegrated and split in several places.

The "white on white" design is created by a technique known as *candlewick*. This is a form of embroidery that typically uses an unbleached cotton thread on a piece of unbleached muslin. The soft spun cotton thread resembles the braided wicks used for candles, hence the name. Motifs were created using a variety of traditional embroidery stitches that included knots, chenille and, as in this case, a tufted stitch.

More popular earlier in the 19th century, this spread includes the date 1854 and the initials M+E in the center of the design. Family lore is that Maria Estey made the quilt just prior to her marriage to James Dickson in Piqua, Ohio in 1854. Her sister Jane wove the cloth, sister Emma spun the tufting fabric, other sisters helped make the coverlet.

White work spreads were fashionable from the Federalist era (1789-1801) to the first quarter of the 19th century and reflected the taste for patriotic and Neo-classical motifs. Eagles were especially popular and are prominently displayed here. Many late 18th and early 19th century quilts were designed with a central medallion. Maria has incorporated this early format but has also included stylistic elements popular in the mid 19th century. The four large pots of flowers are framed much like a central medallion. The surrounding border of birds (eagles in this case) plus fantastical foliage are very similar to motifs found on the red and green four block appliqué quilts so prominent from the 1840s through the 1860s. Maria was familiar with a variety of quilt styles and incorporated them into one textile. (LD)

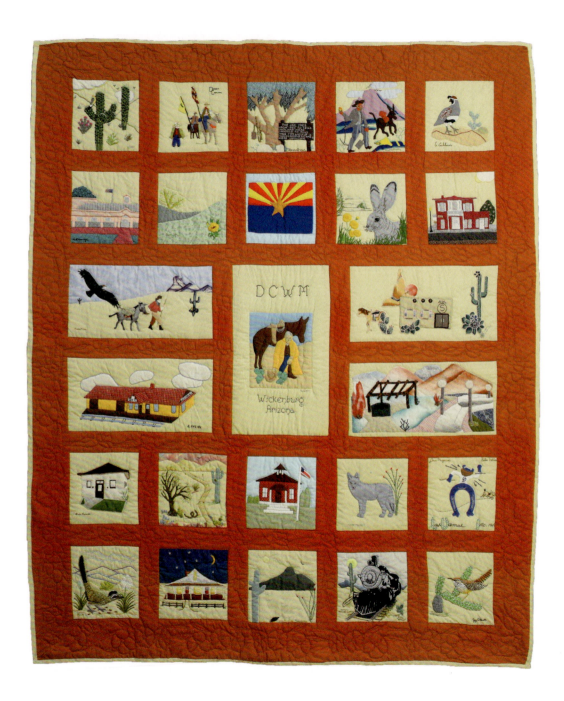

WICKENBURG ALBUM QUILT

1993
Makers: Members of Las Señoras de Socorro Ladies Auxiliary
   of the Maricopa County Historical Society
Batiks, corduroy, cotton, cotton blend, knits, 71" X 83"
Donors: Las Señoras de Socorro; 93.13

The theme of this album quilt is Wickenburg, Arizona and its history. In the introduction to the related coloring book which is available in the museum gift store, the makers explained that they chose to follow the tradition of 19th century album quilts which were "created through a group effort to celebrate special occasions or in commemoration of important events." There are 25 blocks each originally designed by the individual makers. The center medallion block depicts in cloth the bronze sculpture by Joe Beeler named "Thanks for the Rain" which is the showpiece of the museum park.

This quilt was made by women in the Wickenburg area as part of the exhibition *Pieces and Patches* which opened in August 1993. The album blocks depict historical figures, native plants and animals, landmarks, distinctive buildings and events. Each block has a wonderful story such as the Jail Tree which was used in early Wickenburg when the town had no jail house. Important buildings such as the Trinidad House (a military post and stage stop), the Garcia School (1905), the Santa Fe Railway Station (1895) and the Vernetta Hotel are detailed in separate blocks.

Since Wickenburg was known as "The Dude Ranch Capital of the World", a lovely block with dude ranch cacti, mountains and a coyote is included. The Hassayampa River and Wishing Well are also depicted. Of particular interest is the block with an elaborately stitched depiction of Santa Fe engine #761 which dates from 1900.

Western motifs are selectively cut and dimensional appliqué is used in several blocks. Charms and buttons are also utilized by the makers to convey the quilt's story. The batt is a cotton polyester blend. At a quilting bee, it was hand quilted with ten stitches per inch in poppy and vine motifs in the sashing and outline quilting in the blocks. (AH)

WINDMILL BLADES

1925 - 1950
Maker: Francesca Ocampo Quesada
Cottons, 63" x 78.5"
Donors: Josephine Alvarez, Dora, Alicia, Bernard and Eugene Quesada, maker's children; 01.9.2

This is a quilt that grabs your attention; it is practically impossible to look away. For obvious reasons this block is known as "Windmill Blades". Using only two colors – orange and blue – the blades of the windmill seem to literally vibrate and rotate as your eye wanders over the surface. The square in a square block at the corner of each blade adds to the illusion of spinning and whirling. The bright, bold colors are just as appealing to contemporary quilters as they were nearly 70 years ago to the maker of this dazzler.

Family lore is that the daughters assisted their mother in the construction. The blocks are machine pieced and well done. The somewhat thick batting is wool. The body of the quilt is quilted in a fan pattern that belies a fairly unskilled hand. Stitches and width between quilting lines vary and knots are visible on top. The borders are quilted in a hanging diamond pattern, obviously marked without the use of a template. Close inspection reveals that the border uses a slightly different orange than found in the blades of the windmill. Many quilters of varying skill levels were involved in making this quilt. The longer one stares at the quilt the dizzier one becomes. (LD)

THE QUILTS

Arizona Map Quilt 6
Crazy Quilt (Gold Edge) 8
Crazy Quilt (Floral Lining) 10
Crazy Quilt (Maroon/Plum) 12
Crazy Quilt (Wine Velvet) 14
Crazy Quilt Variation / Square in a Square 16
Crown of Thorns 18
Drunkard's Path 20
Embroidered Red Work Summer Spread 22
Embroidered Top 24
Floral Bouquet 26
Four Patch 28
Goose in the Pond 30
Heart Quilt 32
Hen and Chicks/Ducks and Ducklings 34
Jackson Star 36
Lemoyne Star (Carman) 38
Lemoyne Star (Freed) 40
Log Cabin – Courthouse Steps 42
Log Cabin – Straight Furrows 44
Log Cabin – Sunshine and Shadow/Diamonds 46
Lost Ships 48
Many Trips around the World 50
Multi-Colored Silk Triangle Quilt 52
Nine Patch 54
Pink Satin Whole Cloth 56
Poinsettia Appliqué Top 58
Red and Green Appliqué Summer Spread 60
Sawtooth 62
Southern Belle 64
White Work/Candlewick Summer Spread 66
Wickenburg Album Quilt 68
Windmill Blades 70